I0508370

Terms and Conditions

LEGAL NOTICE

The Publisher has strived to be as accurate and complete as possible in the creation of this report, notwithstanding the fact that he does not warrant or represent at any time that the contents within are accurate due to the rapidly changing nature of the Internet.

While all attempts have been made to verify information provided in this publication, the Publisher assumes no responsibility for errors, omissions, or contrary interpretation of the subject matter herein. Any perceived slights of specific persons, peoples, or organizations are unintentional.

In practical advice books, like anything else in life, there are no guarantees of income made. Readers are cautioned to reply on their own judgment about their individual circumstances to act accordingly.

This book is not intended for use as a source of legal, business, accounting or financial advice. All readers are advised to seek services of competent professionals in legal, business, accounting and finance fields.

You are encouraged to print this book for easy reading.

Table Of Contents

Foreword

Chapter 1:
Site Promotion Basics

Chapter 2:
Use Directories

Chapter 3:
Meta Tags And Keywords

Chapter 4:
Build Reader Loyalty

Chapter 5:
Make The Site Easy To Navigate And Use ColorPsychology

Chapter 6:
Build Links

Chapter 7:
Create And Promote A Series For Return Visits

Chapter 8:
Use Network Exchanges

Chapter 9:
Have Awesome Content

Wrapping Up

Foreword

Getting a website up and running is not too difficult to do but ensuring it is done properly in order to optimize traffic interest is the key to a good posting. This is where the promotion of the site comes in only second to that actual site design and content. Get all the info you need here.

Site Promotion Success
Top Tips To Your Site Promotion

Chapter 1:
Site Promotion Basics

Synopsis

Here are some points to consider if one wants to promote a website to ensure optimum results:

The Basics

Putting in some thought and effort is one of the first things the individual should be prepared to do in the quest to promote his or her site. Failing to spend time in this area at the very onset of the whole exercise could prove to be poor decision making.

Understanding and accepting that the process takes time and is an ongoing exercise is important too. Sourcing for information and tips that are current on promotional methods should be done periodically.

Selling something that everyone else is selling may not be the best business endeavor to undertake.

It would be better to choose an element that has very little or no competition at all and allow the search engines to do what they do best which is connect interested parties effectively and quickly.

Designing sites that work properly and efficiently is another point to consider. When the prospect is at the intended site, there is nothing worse that encountering confusing and misleading content.

Contents of this nature will only end up giving the prospect a negative experience and forcing them to leave the site out of frustration.

Making sure the right keywords are used and submitting the site to major search engines is a great and effective promotional tactic.

Use a comprehensive automated submission tool that can properly promote the site at all major search engine platforms. Ensuring the content material is good and accurate will also help to boost the promotional angle of the exercise.

Chapter 2:
Use Directories

Synopsis

Promoting a website is important to ensure the traffic flow to the site is being optimized at all times. Therefore website promotion is an essential part of having and keeping a site relevant and successful.

Directories

One way of effectively doing this is with the use of link directories which come in the form of website directories or article directories.

These tools offer a lot of advantages and are well worth the effort to incorporate into the website, as they help to elevate and improve the search engine listing constantly.

The usual course of action after a site is launch would typically be the search engine spiders going to work cruising the site for the relevant points that usually affect the eventual rankings given.

The indexing and listing results from these visits are then used to facilitate the ranking exercise. Providing as much assistance as possible to these spiders would be an advantage, hence the use of directory links which will lead them straight to the individual's webpage.

Some link directories or article directories use the "no follow" tags which attributes to a share of the Google Page Rank of the webpage where the site or article is published while others will use it to block any PR share, although this can still be made into a straight link for a fee.

The benefits of the link are usually worth the money.

Using the directories links will also facilitate the visitors to such directories easy access to clicking on the links available. Using an anchor text as the main link will sufficiently attract the interest of the visitor so one should ensure the contents of the featured articles are both informative and attention grabbing.

Links that are deep into the websites will provide significant advantages in promoting the entire site in the search engine rather than just at the home page.

Chapter 3:
Meta Tags And Keywords

Synopsis

Site optimization is always a pre requisite of any hopeful new posting and the business, product or service it is promoting. Therefore ensuring all the best possible assistance is given to get the optimization exercise at its peak should be explored for its contributing merits.

Make It Better

There are some that thinks there is really no need to focus on the Meta tags as in their opinions these tags are mostly ignored by the search engines and although there are some merits to the thought process it should nevertheless be explored even for its perceived minimal benefits.

Even though the basic page themes have moved towards more keyword density content, content and linking and a few other beneficial styles there is still come benefits of using the Meta tags.

Meta tag descriptions would have great importance when it comes to determining the positioning of the website on the search results. Usually the number of keywords used and their importance and density within the description tag is pivotal to the manipulation tactics used to heighten the chances of garnering first positioning possibilities.

This is useful as there are still smaller search engines that do focus on using the Meta tag as an evaluation platform.

Keywords are still a very current and powerful tool to ensure optimal search engine rankings. This is will the most obvious exercise that the search engine spiders adopt when cruising the site contents.

This is such an important contributing factor that a lot of sites use chosen keywords that are popular at the time and incorporate them into their own content even if the relevancy factor is not compatible.

However it should also be noted that the over use of the keywords will also create a negative outcome but this is still a point of contention for some.

Therefore choosing keywords that are going to garner the desired attention and attraction to the site is most important and worth exploring.

Chapter 4:
Build Reader Loyalty

Synopsis

The survival of a website depends on many connective features and reader loyalty is one of them. The reader loyalty element is important as it ensure the continued support of the individual thus contributing to the heightened traffic flow to the site which in turn will give rise to the popularity issue of the said site.

Keep Them Coming Back

Basically when there is reader loyalty well established at the site it would mean several things, which may include the site being popular for the contributing content that is both interesting and informative, it would mean that there is interest in the material being posted at the site, it could contribute to the curiosity factor that will eventually encourage other new visitors and many more interesting reasons as to why the site boasts this loyalty.

In order to be able to build such an ideal scenario of reader loyalty some points need to be considered and implemented and the following are just some suggestions to the end:

The interactions are based on tangible benefits. Having good offers and value featured at the sight would effectively be able to garner the interest that can be then converted to consistent visits which will then contribute to forming the reader loyalty base.

Acquiring new customer base through the reader loyalty can also be done when the said reader is encouraged to share the link with others in their own emailing list.

This will effectively widen the reach of the site through the assistance of the current reader loyalty base.

Providing incentives that are significantly helpful to the reader would also encourage the reader to stay loyal to the site.

Facilitating such special offers should ideally be done after some research has been conducted to identify suitable incentives which would not waste the time of the visitor and encourage the continued visits for the content and the incentives featured.

Chapter 5:

Make The Site Easy To Navigate And Use Color Psychology

Synopsis

Being able to strike a comfortable balance in the designing and content of a site is important to eventual result and the corresponding reception it is going to receive from the viewing target audience. Therefore incorporating elements such as good navigation and color psychology are important and essential to the design of the site.

Make It Simple

However in doing so the individual should be careful not to overwhelm the target audience with nice to look at pages that are not navigation friendly or easy to navigate pages with poorly designed content.

Both pose some negativity and thus should be avoided at all costs. Having noted this, the task of incorporating both the easy navigation and the color into a site design and content should not be overly confusing, difficult or stressful.

Providing an attractive menu that empowers the user with an easy to follow navigation will encourage them to feel comfortable and excited to access the information as they go along.

Positioning the navigation in the same areas on all pages and using different fonts and colors is also advised. The general rule of thumb would be to ensure the visitor does not have to go around in circles clicking on links that end up not giving them what they were seeking in the first place and even worse frustrating them so much that they make up their mind not to visit the site again.

The use of colors especially if they are pleasing and subtle will play on the physic perception of the viewer. However if there is a need to drive home a dynamic point then perhaps the use of more vibrant colors may be needed.

Color have long been an attention grabbing tool that is widely used in advertising platforms thus using them wisely for web designs is also something to consider.

Chapter 6:
Build Links

Synopsis

Link building is an aspect of the online engine that should not be disregarded as unnecessary and cumbersome. In actual fact a website that intents to reach the masses cannot afford to overlook this important tool for its traffic enhancement attributes.

Links

There are a few reasons why the link building should be given due consideration and the following are just some to be explored:

Being one of the more powerful methods of effectively and properly delivering information to those seeking something from a particular niche area is one of the more dominant features it boasts.

Ideally the links should be consistent with the material at the original host's site but there are some although relatively few cases where the links are not related.

Including quality content in the sites linked will eventually help to create the credibility for the site and this feature is a highly regarded one within the more serious prospects to any site.

Even the search engines favor sites with credible content and links this contributing to the positive parameters engaged by the search engine methodology.

As a result of the credibility, trust and excitement build over the content issue, the influx of inbound links will contribute to more attention being given to the site by search engines.

This of course will also positively contribute to the reevaluation of the rankings, to better placements.

All this link building exercises will also contribute positively to the sales and profit revenue that can be harnessed from the heightened activity caused by the links.

The increased visibility factor facilitated by the links would definitely contribute to the possibility. These actions could cover a vast range of activity such as purchases, interactive participation, forums, blogs and many others, which in turn would bring about even more interest in the site through further related links.

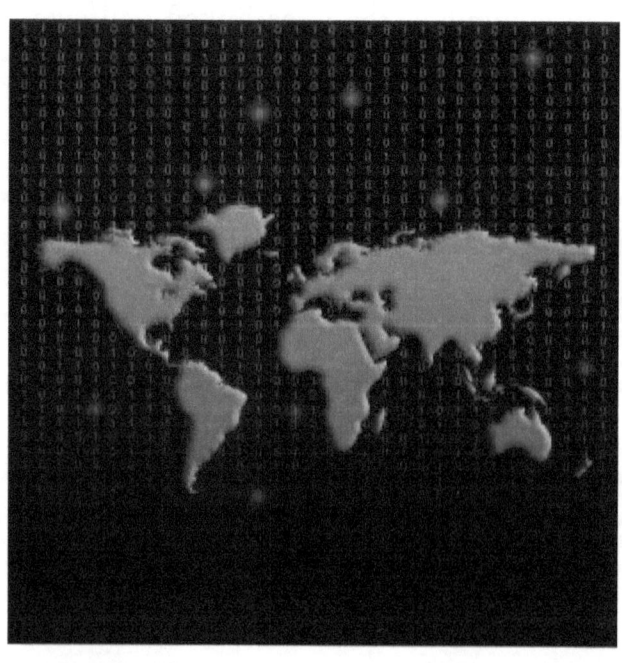

Chapter 7:

Create And Promote A Series For Return Visits

Synopsis

After the initial visit to the site, all steps should be taken to ensure the visitor continues to revisit the site regularly and consistently. This is done using a number of innovative ways, some of which are explored below:

Drum Up Interest

- Providing new information in the content is important as interested parties will only revisit the site if they are assured of finding fresh information, ideas, post and other helpful features at the site. Therefore there is always a need to stay informed in the area chosen so that one can provide such new information for the site's content matter.

- Creating avenues for the availability of the new postings at the site is also needed. Alerts and other forms prompting and informing the target audience of the new material available is equally important as some may not be aware of the new features thus fail to visit the site.

- Regularly conducting updating exercises at the site would also help to encourage the visitors to return to the site as they would be assured of not having to view outdated information which will in turn create the perceived authority on the subject matter posted. The visitors would then be firmly convinced that all the latest information can be gotten from this particular site based on the updating exercise that is periodically conducted.

- Conducting an analytical observation exercise on the visitors' statistics and their more obvious interest and searches will also allow the individual to make a more informed decision on what

to feature at his or her site. Featuring content material that is relevant will definitely ensure return visits as the participants would have already been actively interested in sourcing such material as part of their searching agenda.

- Also one should always ensure that besides featuring new material periodically one should also ensure that the visitor is "taken" the new material easily through clearly shown links.

Chapter 8:
Use Network Exchanges

Synopsis

Staying competitive is always a priority when it comes to keeping the site relevant. In trying to do so the individual needs to be constantly and actively looking for new information to be sourced, designed and featured at his or her site.

This can prove to be an uphill battle especially for those with time constraints. However with the existence of the network exchange platform this problem may have found its solution.

Networking

The exchange network is designed to provide information or site content through more effective and efficient channels whereby information is disseminated and shared among interested parties.

This approach of sourcing and providing information is now gaining popularity for more reasons than just being able to eliminate the individual's need to be tied to performing these exercises for themselves.

Another beneficial use of the network exchange is that a variety of viewpoints can be accessed though this method. Instead of having just the information based on the views and efforts of one person, the exchange exercise facilitates the platform to be effectively boundless thus providing surprisingly more innovative contents based on other points of view.

This is also especially useful if the other participants are more technologically sound in their content contribution and can provide irrefutable information.

Tapping into this will further enhance the trustworthy element tagged to the individual's site as the content is acquired for reliable sources.

Financially this could also be an advantage as pooled resources shared are better than having to get everything done alone. This method of network exchange also encourages interactive developments which in turn can lead to other branched out content possibilities.

The exercise of researching and gathering information can often be a rather tedious and stressful exercise therefore having the network exchange tool creates the better spreading out of the work load in a more manageable way.

Chapter 9:
Have Awesome Content

Synopsis

In the quest to create a site that stands above the rest exploring the possibilities of providing awesome content can be an option to look into.

As every site on the internet is going to be providing similar information on related topics, the individual should take the trouble to design the site to feature awesome material.

The Content

Here are some benefits to considering featuring awesome content at the website:

Wider search engine profile is about quantifying the traffic flow using the search engine bots through the profile exercise which can be done with awesome material content.

By increasing the level of the content to simply awesome, the traffic flow to the site can be phenomenal.

Making research and quality information a priority when sourcing for content material will eventually ideally create the platform for awesome content.

This content can then be featured at the site, where it will be identified as deserving of higher ranking based on quality work designed.

When the search engine does this there is an automatic positive reaction from the viewing parties whereby they would focus more on such sites when surfing.

Fresh, new and exciting concepts when introduced at the site will be considered an awesome element especially if the idea is practical and beneficial.

Providing such awesome content periodically will create the excitement that drives the traffic to the site thus effectively creating a "buzz" around the site.

Awesome material content can also create a good amount of referrals which is very good for the site.

The viewers who visit the site will encourage others to do the same based on the information content that they themselves enjoyed viewing and found to be informative and beneficial.

This form of advertising is something money cannot buy and is the ultimate way of gaining recognition for the site featured.

Wrapping Up

For those who venture into the online internet marketing arena, understanding that all does not unfold instantaneously and positively is pivotal in keeping them in the game. Patience and perseverance is something that should be part of the makeup of the individual otherwise the foray into this field will be short and disastrous.

Being patient when attempting to produce a winning website is a good characteristic to have especially when most new comers are all fired up and ready to charge head on into the designing and creating part of the exercise.

This would lead to an enthusiasm that if left uncurbed could cause detrimental effects to the designing part of the whole experience.

Although enthusiasm is a good thing to have, too much of it will contribute to the individual trying to put too many items into the content material which would ultimately end up confusing the viewer.

When problems arise which they inventibly will the individual have to have the reserves to tap into in order to keep the perseverance real and continuous. Sometimes this may mean having to revamp the whole site from content to design and maybe even topic choice.

Though this may prove to be difficult for those who perceive their work as being faultless, it is still a necessary tack to carry out.

Perhaps the content featured at the time was not what the prospect were looking for thus overlooking the site altogether. It does not always mean that the site itself is poorly designed or posted.

Through the experience of trial and error the individual is also able to acquire valuable experience along the way which may prove to be an asset in the long run.

The experience will also arm the individual with the information that could be used in the future should it be deemed beneficial, necessary or current.

www.ingramcontent.com/pod-product-compliance
Lightning Source LLC
Chambersburg PA
CBHW030551220526
45463CB00007B/3061